LITTLE BOOK
⇒ OF ⇒
HEDGEHOGS

WEIDENFELD & NICOLSON
LONDON

BIRDS & BEASTIES
Barbara Briggs

HEDGEHOG

Twitching the leaves where the drainpipe clogs
   In ivy leaves and mud, a purposeful
Creature at night is about his business. Dogs
   Fear his stiff seriousness. He chews away

At beetles, worms, slugs, frogs. Can kill a hen
   With one snap of his jaws, can taunt a snake
To death on muscled spines. Old countrymen
   Tell tales of hedgehogs sucking a cow dry.

But this one, cramped by houses, fences, walls,
   Must have slept here all winter in that heap
Of compost, or have inched by intervals
   Through tidy gardens to this ivy bed.

A country creature, wary, quiet and shrewd,
   He takes the milk we give him, when we're gone.
At night, our slamming voices must seem crude
   To one who sits and waits for silence.

from HEDGEHOG
Anthony Thwaite

HEDGEHOG MYSTERY

This wanderer of hedgerow, lane
　　And wood, this spiny hog,
Comes gently, snuffling, once again,
　　Emerges from the fog
Of centuries bygone, of dreams,
　　And curls before our sight,
And smoke-like, grave and secret seems
　　This denizen of night.
Yet charm as ever conquers all,
　　As caring holds the key
To woodland haunt, to coarse brown ball,
　　To hedgehog mystery!

HEDGEHOG MYSTERY
Frank Marples

HEDGEHOG

T. Pennant

Ball of Spears

The hedgehog from its hollow root
Sees the wood moss clear of snow
And hunts each hedge for fallen fruit
Crab hip and winter bitten sloe
And oft when checked by sudden fears
As shepherd dog his haunts espies
He rolls up in a ball of spears
And all his barking rage defies.

from FEBRUARY – A THAW
John Clare 1793–1864

A PRICKLY PROBLEM
George Augustus Holmes

The Hedgehog's Secret

The snail moves like a
Hovercraft, held up by a
Rubber cushion of itself,
Sharing its secret

With the hedgehog. The hedgehog
Shares its secret with no one.
We say, Hedgehog, come out
Of yourself and we will love you.

We mean no harm. We want
Only to listen to what
You have to say. We want
Your answers to our questions.

The hedgehog gives nothing
Away, keeping itself to itself.
We wander what a hedgehog
Has to hide, why it so distrusts.

We forget the god
Under the crown of thorns.
We forget that never again
Will a god trust in the world.

HEDGEHOG
Paul Muldoon

MRS TIGGY-WINKLE HIDES THE
KEY UNDER THE DOOR-SILL
Beatrix Potter

HEDGEHOGS

The Tale of
Mrs Tiggy-Winkle

er print gown was tucked up, she was wearing a large apron over her striped petticoat. Her little black nose went sniffle, sniffle, snuffle, and her eyes went twinkle, twinkle; and underneath her cap – where Lucie had yellow curls – that little person had PRICKLES!...

She was running running running up the hill – and where was her white frilled cap? and her shawl? and her gown – and her petticoat?

And *how* small she had grown – and *how* brown – and covered with PRICKLES!

Why! Mrs Tiggy-Winkle was nothing but a HEDGEHOG.

from THE TALE OF
MRS TIGGY-WINKLE
Beatrix Potter 1866–1943

HEDGEHOGS

SCISSORSPINE

—————— • ——————

There's a hedgehog in our garden,
He's only made of clay,
But at least I know for certain –
He'll never go away.
The other Hedgehog – (Scissorspine)
Well, he just comes and goes,
He makes a funny shuffling sound
With his little pointed nose.
So the Hedgehog I like best
Is the one who *doesn't* stay,
He eats my sliced banana
And then he goes away!

Mrs Alex Richards

HEDGEHOG AND A
FIELDMOUSE IN A HEDGEROW
WITH FALLEN APPLES
Lesley Fotherby

from The Natural
History of Animals
Friedrich Specht 1887

HEDGEHOGS

Little Round Holes

H edge-hogs abound in my garden and fields. The manner in which they eat their roots of plantain in my grass-walks is very curious: with their upper mandible, which is much longer than their lower, they bore under the plant, and so eat the root off upwards, leaving the tuft of leaves untouched. In this respect they are very serviceable, as they destroy a very troublesome weed; but they deface the walks by some measure by digging little round holes. It appears by the dung that they drop upon the turf, that beetles are no inconsiderable part of their food.

from THE NATURAL HISTORY
OF SELBORNE
Gilbert White 1720–1793

PARNASSUS
Andrea Montegna 1431–1506

BE NOT SEEN

*Y*ou spotted snakes, with double tongues,
　Thorny hedge-hogs, be not seen;
Newts and bind-worms do not wrong;
　Come not near our fairy queen.

from A MIDSUMMER
NIGHT'S DREAM
William Shakespeare 1564–1616

HEDGEHOG AND YOUNG

Louis Sargent 1909

Little Snout

The hedgehog is a little beast
  Who likes a quiet wood,
Where he can feed his family
  On proper hedgehog food.

He has a funny little snout
  That's rather like a pig's,
With which he smells, like us,
    of course,
  But also runts and digs.

He wears the queerest prickle coat,
  Instead of hair or fur,
And only has to curl himself
  To bristle like a burr.

He does not need to battle with
  Or run away from foes,
His coat does all the work for him,
  It pricks them on the nose.

THE HEDGEHOG
Edith King

HEDGEHOGS

HEDGEHOG WISDOM

The fox knows many things
the hedgehog one big one.

Archilochus

c.680-640 BC

*from Alice's Adventures
in Wonderland
Gwynedd M. Hudson*

THE HEDGEHOG
from The Naturalist's Library 1835

The Cinderpath

'A hedgehog is a creature with four legs, and thorns.'
That's what the roadman said,
So when I found one ambling uncertainly
On ridiculous, small feet, along the way
That's lined with dandelions and deadnettles
I thought: 'There's a hedgehog!
I wonder if he'll stay?'

We put out milk in a saucer.
Night by night
It disappeared. But we never saw him take it
Until I came swiftly
In pyjamas
Treading on each stair carefully
Not to creak it –

And there he was, not one, but with a trickle
Of wife and children wobbling after him
Scuffing their feet in the dark, wet grass.
I watched him then
Nuzzling and snuffling at the saucer's brim
With a soft, sweet, suckling sound…

Next time I pass
Near the cinderpath with the dandelions
I shall look
For a creature with four legs, and thorns growing on it,
Wambling along like a hedge with no rose in it.
I might even write about him
In a book.

THE COMPOSITION
Jean Kenward

HEDGEHOG HEAVEN

*T*he only indication of a belief in a future state which I ever detected in an old Gypsy woman, was that she once dreamed she was in heaven. It appeared to her as a large garden full of fine fat hedgehogs.

Richard Liebich writing about
Gypsies in 1863

A FOREST FLOOR

Matthias Withoos 1627–1703

PUZZLED *Philip Eustace Stretton* fl.1884-1919

HEDGEHOGS

At the Bottom of the Garden

✦

*N*o, it isn't an old football
grown all shrunken and prickly
because it was left out so long
at the bottom of the garden

It's only Miss Hedgehog
who, when she thinks I'm not looking,
unballs herself to move…
  like bristling black lightning.

AT THE BOTTOM OF THE GARDEN
Grace Nichols

27

HEDGEHOGS

LITTLE PIGS

In June last I procured a litter of four or five young hedge-hogs, which appeared to be about five or six days old…No doubt their spines are soft and flexible at the time of their birth, or else the poor dam would have but a bad time of it in the critical moment of parturition: but it is plain that they soon harden; for these little pigs have stiff prickles on their backs and sides as would easily have fetched blood, had they not been handled with caution…They can, in part, at this age draw their skin down over their faces; but are not able to contract themselves into a ball, as they do, for the sake of defence, when full grown. The reason, I suppose, is because of the curious muscle that enables the creature to roll itself up into a ball was not then arrived at its full tone and firmness.

from THE NATURAL HISTORY OF SELBORNE
Gilbert White 1720–1793

FAMILY OF HEDGHOGS

Seigmar Jugelt b.1954

OLD MR PRICKLEPIN

Beatrix Potter 1866–1943

HEDGEHOGS

Little Holly Hedgehog

L ittle Holly Hedgehog
Went for a stroll one night
To call and see her cousins
Because the moon was bright.

But first she had her supper
A big fat juicy worm.
She found it and she gobbled it
Before that worm could turn!

Then off she went at quite a rate,
Across the garden through the gate,
Over the road and into the field
Along the hedgerow high,
And all the while the little stars
Were twinkling in the sky.

Soon she found her cousins' nest –
But to her dismay,
A passing field mouse told her
They'd gone on holiday!

So little Holly Hedgehog
Explored a bit and then
When the dawn was breaking,
Went back home again.

LITTLE HOLLY HEDGEHOG
Nadia Garsed

Hedgehog Be Careful

Watch out watch out
Hedgehog on the road
Careful all those lorries
With their heavy load

Hedgehog Hedgehog
Careful in the lane
Remember the big lorries?
Well here they come again

Careful when you're crossing
Rabbit, Frog or Toad
Remember little Hedgehog
There's danger on the road

There's the sorry Pussy
Got run over flat
So careful little Hedgehog
Or you'll end up a mat.

HEDGEHOG
Spike Milligan

CARICATURE OF JOHANNES BRAHMS

Otto Böhler

from *The Hedgehog Feast*
Edith Holden

HEDGEHOGS

PINCUSHION FRIEND

*E*lderly, dignified, cautious and wise,
Is Potto our hedgehog whose bright jewel eyes
Twinkle with whimsical humour when we,
Forgiving his manners, invite him to tea.
I have a suspicion he views us with scorn
As he scampers and grunts in the night on the lawn.
But I think he approves of us humans by day,
Through his saucer of milk and nest of rolled hay.
How kindly it is of Dear Nature to send
Such a sensible, lovable pincushion friend.

J M G Halsted

HEDGEHOGS

HEDGEHOG STRIFE

The hedgehog hides beneath the rotten hedge
And makes a great round nest of grass and sedge
Or in a bush or in a hollow tree
And many often stoops and say they see
Him roll and fill his prickles full of crabs
And creep away and where the magpies dabs
His wing at muddy dyke in aged root
He makes a nest and fills it full of fruit
On the hedge bottom hunts for crabs and sloes
And whistles like a cricket as he goes
It rolls up like a ball or shapeless hog
When gipseys hunt it with their noisy dogs
Ive seen it in their camps they call it sweet
Though black and bitter and unsavoury meat
But they who hunt the field for rotten meat
And wash the muddy dyke and call it sweat*
And eat what dogs refuse where ere they dwell
Care little either for the taste or smell
They say they milk the cows and when they lye
Nibble their fleshy teats and make them dry

sweet

36

from The Royal Natural History
ed. R. Lydekker 1896

But they whove seen the small head like a hog
Rolled up to meet the savage of a dog
With mouth scarce big enough to hold a straw
Will neer believe what no one ever saw
But still they hunt the hedges all about
And shepherd dogs are trained to hunt them out
They hurl with savage force the stick and stone
And no one cares and still the strife goes on.

THE HEDGEHOG
John Clare 1793–1864

HEDGEHOGS

Mr Hedgehog

The owls have feathers lined with down
To keep them nice and warm;
The rats have top-coats soft and brown
To wrap in from the storm;
And nearly every bird and beast
Has cosy suits to wear,
But Mr Hedgehog has the least
Of any for his share.

His back is stuck with prickly pins
That breezes whistle through,
And when the winter-time begins
The only thing to do
Is just to find a leafy spot,
And curl up from the rain,
Until the Spring comes, bright and hot,
To waken him again.

HEDGEHOG

A. Thorburn 1920

The owls and rats and all their folk
Are soft and smooth to touch,
But hedgehogs are not nice to stroke,
Their prickles hurt so much.
So, though it looks a little queer,
His coat is best of all;
For nobody could interfere
With such a bristly ball!

THE HEDGEHOG AND HIS COAT

Elizabeth Fleming

HEDGEHOGS

By Thorny Dykes

Thou grimmest far o grusome tykes
Gubbin thy food by thorny dykes
Gude faith, thou disnawant for pikes
  Baith sharp an rauckle;*
Thou looks (Lord save's) arrayed in spikes,
  A creepin heckle.

Sure Nick begat thee, at the first,
On some auld whin or thorn accurst;
An some horn-figured harpie nurst
  The ugly urchin;
Then Belzie, laughin' like to burst,
  First caad thee Hurchin.**

Fowk tell how thou, sal far frae daft,
Whan wind-faan fruit be scattered saft,
Will row thysel wi cunning craft
  And bear awa
Upon thy back, what fares thee aft,
  A day or twa.

TO A HEDGEHOG
Samuel Thompson 1766–1816

* strong

** hedgehog

THE HEDGEHOG

Deirdre Mackay Clarke

WILD LIFE SERIES – HEDGEHOG

Sue Warner

HEDGEHOGS

FRIEND

Over the grass a hedgehog came
Questing the air for scents of food
And the cracked twig of danger.
He shuffled near in the gloom. Then stopped.
He was aware of me. I went up,
Bent low to look at him, and saw
His coat of lances pointing to my hand.
What could I do
To show I was no enemy?
I turned him over, inspected his small clenched paws,
His eyes expressionless as glass,
And did not know how I could speak,
By tongue or touch, the language of a friend.

from HEDGEHOG IN AIR RAID
Clifford Dyment

HEDGEHOGS

ASLEEP

*T*he Hedgehog sleeps beneath the hedge –
As you may sometimes see –
And I prefer it sleeping there
To sleeping here with me!

THE HEDGEHOG

J. J. Bell

FORAGING

Hilary Jones

DRÔLERIE

von Gautier de Metz

HEDGEHOGS

Take My Quills

'Give me of your quills, O Hedgehog!
All your quills, O Kagh, the Hedgehog!
I will make a necklace of them,
Make a girdle for my beauty,
And two stars to deck her bosom!'

From a hollow tree the Hedgehog
With his sleepy eyes looked at him,
Shot his shining quills like arrows,
Saying, with a drowsy murmur,
Through the tangle of his whiskers:
'Take my quills, O Hiawatha!'

from THE SONG OF HIAWATHA
Henry Wadsworth Longfellow 1807–1882

HEDGEHOGS

BUNCH-O'-SPEARS

But best of all the Folk-with-Fears
That walk when dusk is down
I love the little Bunch-o'-Spears,
So businesslike and brown,
That pads along the trodden track
Alert yet undismayed,
With all his armour on his back
And every point displayed.

When he and I walk side by side
Beneath the shadow's screen
He leaves, as levelly we stride,
A courteous space between;
And as the cars dash past unslowed
The thought occurs to me
That there are hogs upon the road
Less likeable than he.

THE HEDGEHOG
W. H. Ogilvie

HEDGEHOG BOOKPLATE

LE HÉRISSON

mid-19th century

HEDGEHOGS

Prickly Friend

I do like hedges, that is true,
But I am not a pig, so why do you
Call me a hog, which is a bit of a boar,
And I'd prefer if you didn't anymore.
Prickly friend would be more correct,
For punctured skin you can expect.
Come too close and I'll roll in a ball
And you won't be able to touch me at all.
Yes, prickly friend is a better word,
But to call me a hog is just absurd.

PRICKLY FRIEND
Isaac Stewart

HEDGEHOGS

Hedgehog Croquet

Alice thought she had never seen such a curious croquet-game in all her life; it was all ridges and furrows; the balls were live hedgehogs, the mallets live flamingoes, and the soldiers had to double themselves up and to stand upon their hands and feet to make the arches.

The chief difficulty Alice found at first was managing her flamingo...when she had got its head down, and was going to begin again, it was very provoking to find that the hedgehog had unrolled itself, and was in the act of crawling away...Alice soon came to the conclusion that it was a very difficult game indeed.

from ALICE'S ADVENTURES
IN WONDERLAND
Lewis Carroll 1832–1898

from Alice's Adventures in Wonderland

Gwynedd M. Hudson

from The Hedgehog Feast
Edith Holden

HEDGEHOGS

BE MY VALENTINE

*G*one are the passions, the tears and the joys
Of yesterday's romances, sweethearts and boys.
I remember the letters, the poems, the proses,
The 'phone calls, the outings, the chocolates, the roses.
But dearer to me than the prettiest posey
Is the dew drop that hangs from your little wet nosey.
Reclusive, illusive, wandering nightly,
Unprickle the charms that you've rolled up so tightly.
You shy little treasure, I wish you were mine,
I wish you would love me, be *my* Valentine.
Please stay here and share my life, don't go away,
Oh wild one, dear Hedgehog, my love of today.

BE MY VALENTINE
Elaine Drewery

HEDGEHOGS

Acknowledgements

British Library Cataloguing in Publication Data. A
catalogue record for this book is available from the
British Library.

Designed and created by
THE BRIDGEWATER BOOK COMPANY
Words chosen by JOANNE JESSOP
Picture research by FELICITY COX *and* VANESSA
FLETCHER
Page make-up by JANE LANAWAY
Printed in Italy

*The publishers wish to thank the following for
the use of pictures:*
ARCHIV FÜR KUNST AND GESCHICHTE,
London: p.33; Bibliothèque Nationale, Paris p.46;
Musée du Louvre, Paris pp.16–17. BRIDGEMAN ART
LIBRARY: pp.42, 45; British Library p.9; Chris
Beetles pp.13, 41; Josef Mensing Gallery p.29. J.L.
CHARMET, Paris: Bibliothèque des Arts Décoratifs
p.50. CHRISTIES IMAGES: back cover, pp.6–7, 25.
E.T. ARCHIVE: British Museum p.5. FINE ART
PHOTOGRAPHIC LIBRARY: pp.26–7. Reproduced by
permission of FREDERICK WARNE & CO.: p.10
(Copyright © Frederick Warne & Co., 1905, 1987),
p.30 (Copyright © Frederick Warne & Co., 1917,
1987). MARY EVANS PICTURE LIBRARY: front cover,
title page, pp.2, 18–19, 22. NATURAL HISTORY
MUSEUM: p.39. Illustration by Edith Holden
reproduced from *The Hedgehog Feast*. Author
Rowena Stott. Copyright © Richard Webb Limited
1978: pp.34, 54. SOTHEBY'S TRANSPARENCY
LIBRARY: p.49.

*The publishers gratefully acknowledge permission
to reproduce the following material in this book:*
p.3 *Hedgehog* by Anthony Thwaite from *Anthony
Thwaite Poems 1953–1983* published by Century
Hutchinson Ltd; by permission of Anthony Thwaite.
p.4 *Hedgehog Mystery*
by permission of the author. pp.8–9 *The Hedgehog*
from *New Weather* by Paul Muldoon by permission
of Faber and Faber Ltd. p.11 *The Tale of Mrs Tiggy-
Winkle* by Beatrix Potter © Frederick Warne &
Co., 1905; by permission of Frederick Warne and
Co. p.12 By permission of the author. pp.22-23 *The
Composition* by Jean Kenward from *Of Caterpillars,
Cats and Cattle* (Viking Kestrel, 1987); by permission
of Penguin Books. p.27 *At the Bottom of the Garden* by
Grace Nichols from *Prickly Poems* published by
Hutchinson Children's Books, 1992. p.31 *Little
Holly Hedgehog* by permission of the author. p.32
Hedgehog by Spike Milligan from *Prickly Poems*
published by Hutchinson Children's Books, 1992.
p.35 By permission of the author. p.43 *Hedgehog in
Air Raid* by Clifford Dyment By permission of the
copyright holder, Irene Dyment, and her agent,
Classic Presentations Ltd. p.51 *Prickly Friend* by
permission of the author. p.55 *Be My Valentine* by
permission of the author.

*Every effort has been made to trace all copyright
holders and obtain permissions. The editor
and publishers sincerely apologise for any
inadvertent errors or omissions and will be
happy to correct them in any future edition.*